by John Updike

POETRY

THE CARPENTERED HEN *(1958)*

TELEPHONE POLES *(1963)*

MIDPOINT *(1969)*

SHORT STORIES

THE SAME DOOR *(1959)*

PIGEON FEATHERS *(1962)*

OLINGER STORIES: *A Selection (1964)*

THE MUSIC SCHOOL *(1966)*

NOVELS

THE POORHOUSE FAIR *(1959)*

RABBIT, RUN *(1960)*

THE CENTAUR *(1963)*

OF THE FARM *(1965)*

COUPLES *(1968)*

ESSAYS

ASSORTED PROSE *(1965)*

MIDPOINT

and Other Poems

John Updike

MIDPOINT
and Other Poems

Alfred A. Knopf · New York

1969

THIS IS A BORZOI BOOK
PUBLISHED BY ALFRED A. KNOPF, INC.

ACKNOWLEDGMENTS

Some of these poems were previously published in *The New Republic, Harper's Magazine, The Atlantic Monthly, The American Scholar, Look, Polemic, Première, The Saturday Review* and *The Transatlantic Review*. The following poems first appeared in *The New Yorker:* "Fireworks," "Dream Objects," "The Angels," "Some Frenchmen," "Farewell to the Shopping District of Antibes," "Exposé," "Postcards From Soviet Cities," "Antigua," "Sea Knell," and "Report of Health." "Dog's Death" was originally printed as a broadside sheet by the Adams House and Lowell House Printers at Harvard University. Canto III of "Midpoint" is closely based upon the September 1967 issue of *The Scientific American* and appears in the January 1969 issue of that magazine. The Whitman lines in Canto IV are all from "Song of Myself."

CONTENTS

CONTENTS

Light Verse

Midpoint

I. INTRODUCTION

ARGUMENT: The poet begins, and describes his beginnings. Early intimations of wonder and dread. His family on the Hill of Life *circa* 1942, and his own present uncomfortable maturity. Refusing to take good advice, he insists on the endurance of the irreducible.

Of nothing but me, me
—all wrong, all wrong—
as I cringe in the face of glory

I sing, lacking another song.
Proud mouths around me clack
that the livelong day is long

but the nip of night tugs back
my would-be celebrant brain
to the bricks of the moss-touched walk,

the sweet cold grass that had no name,
the arbor, and the wicker chair
turned cavernous beneath the tapping rain.

Plain wood and paint pressed back my stare.
Stiff cardboard apples crayoned to sell
(for nickels minted out of air)

from orange crates with still a citrus smell:
the thermometer: the broom:
this code of things contrived to tell

a timid God of a continuum
wherein he was enchanted.
Vengeful, he applied his sense of doom

with tricycle tires to coppery-red
anthills and, dizzy in his Heaven, grieved
his crushed Inferno of the dead.

A screen of color said, *You are alive.*
A skin of horror floated at my feet.
The corpses, comma-shaped, indicted, *If*

a wheel from far above (in summer heat,
loose thunders roamed the sky like untongued wagons)
would turn, you'd lie squashed on the street.

That bright side porch in Shillington:
under the sun, beneath grape leaves,
I feared myself an epiphenomenon.

The crucial question was, *Why am I me?*
In China boys were born as cherishing
of their small selves; in buried Greece

their swallowed spirits wink
like mica lost in marble.
Sickened by Space's waste, I tried to cling

to the thought of the indissoluble:
a point infinitely hard
was luminous in me, and cried *I will.*

I sought in middling textures part-
icles of iridescence, scintillae
in dullish surfaces; and pictured art

as descending, via pencil, into dry
exactitude. The beaded curtain
of Matter hid an understanding Eye.

Clint Shilling's drawing lessons: in
the sun he posed an egg on paper, and said
a rainbow ran along the shadow's rim—

the rainbow at the edge of the shadow of the egg.
My kindergarten eyes were sorely strained
to see it there. My still-soft head

began to ache, but docilely I feigned
the purple ghosts of green in clumsy wax:
thus was I early trained

and wonder, now, if Clint were orthodox.
He lived above a spikestone-studded wall
and honed his mustache like a tiny ax

and walked a brace of collies down our alley
in Pennsylvania dusk
beside his melodic wife, white-haired and tall.

O Philadelphia Avenue! My eyes lift up
from the furtive pencilled paper
and drown, are glad to drown, in a flood

of light, of trees and houses: our neighbors
live higher than we, in gaunt
two-family houses glaring toward our arbor.

Five-fingered leaves hold horsechestnuts.
The gutter runs with golden water
from Flickinger's iceplant. Telephone wires hunt

through the tree-crowns under orders
to find the wider world
the daily *Eagle* and the passing autos

keep hinting the existence of. And girls
stroll toward Lancaster Avenue and school
in the smoke of burning leaves, in the swirl

of snow, in the cruel
brilliance that follows, in the storm of buds that marries
earth to the iron sky and brings renewal

to the town so wide and fair from quarry
to trolley tracks, from Kenhorst to Mohnton,
from farmers' market to cemetery,

that a boy might feel himself point O
in optics, where plane ABCD—
a visual phenomenon—

converges and passes through to be
(inverted on the other side,
where film or retina receive it)

a kind of afterlife,
knife-lifted out of flux
and developed out of time:

the night sky, with a little luck,
was a camera back, the constellations
faint silver salts, and I the crux

of radii, the tip of two huge cones,
called Heaven and Earth,
that took their slant and spin from me alone.

I was that O, that white-hot nothing, yet
my hands, my penis, came also into view,
and as I grew I half unwilling learned

to seem a creature, to subdue
my giant solipsism to a common scale.
Reader, it is enchanting to share with you

the plight of love, the fate
of death, the need for food,
the privileges of ignorance, the ways

of traffic, competition, and remorse.
I look upon my wife, and marvel that
a woman, competent and good,

has shared my years; my children, protein-fat,
echo my eyes and my laugh: I am disarmed
to think that my body has mattered,

has been enrolled like a red-faced farm-
boy in the beautiful country club
of mankind's copulating swarm.

I did not expect it; humble
as a glow-worm, my boneless ego asked
only to witness, to serve as the hub

of a wheeling spectacle that would not pass.
My parents, my impression was,
had acted out all parts on my behalf;

their shouting and their silences
in the hissing bedroom dark
scorched the shadows; a ring of ashes

expanded with each smoldering remark
and left no underbrush of fuel
of passion for my intimidated spark.

My mother's father squeezed his Bible
sighing, and smoked five-cent cigars
behind the chickenhouse, exiling the smell.

His wife, bespectacled Granma,
beheaded the chickens
in their gritty wire yard

and had a style of choking during dinner;
she'd run to the porch, where one of us
would pound her on the back until her inner

conflict had resolved. Like me, she was nervous;
I had sympathetic stomach cramps.
We were, perhaps, too close,

the five of us. Our lamps
were dim, our carpets worn, the furniture
hodgepodge and venerable and damp.

And yet I never felt that we were poor.
Our property included several stray
cats, one walnut tree, a hundred yards or more

of privet hedge, and fresh ice every other day.
The brothers pressing to be born
were kept, despite their screams, offstage.

The fifth point of a star, I warmed
to my role, threw tantrums,
and catered to the others for applause.

How old was I when to amuse them
I drew the Hill of Life?
My grandfather, then seventy-some,

is near the bottom, beside
a Heavenly sunset, though twenty years
in fact would pass before he, ninety, died,

of eating an unwashed peach.
His wife, crippled but chipper, stepped
above him downward and, true, did not precede

him into that sunset, but snored and slept
six seasons more before her speechless spirit
into unresisted silence crept.

A gap, and then my father, Mr.
Downdike of high-school hilarity,
strides manful down the inexplicably unslippery

pencil line. My mother is at the peak—
perhaps she was thirty-five—
and starting up the lonely upslope is me,

dear Chonny, maybe ten. Now on the downward side
behold me: my breath is short,
though my parents are still alive.

For conscientious climbing, God gave me these rewards:
fame with its bucket of unanswerable letters,
wealth with its worrisome market report,

rancid advice from my critical betters,
a drafty house, a voluptuous spouse,
and *quatre enfants*—none of them bed-wetters.

From *Time*'s grim cover, my fretful face peers out.
Ten thousand soggy mornings have warped my lids
and minced a crafty pulp of this my mouth;

and yet, incapable of being dimmed,
there harbors still inside me like the light
an anchored ketch displays, among my ribs,

a hopeful burning riding out the tide
that this strange universe employs
to strip itself of wreckage in the night.

"Take stock. Repent. The motion that destroys
creates elsewhere; the looping sun
sees no world twice." False truths! I vouch for boys

impatient, inartistically, to get things done,
armored in speckled cardboard
and an untoward faith in the eye/I pun.

II. THE PHOTOGRAPHS

ARGUMENT: The pictures speak for themselves. A cycle of growth, mating, and birth. The coarse dots, calligraphic and abstract, become faces, with troubled expressions. Distance improves vision. Lost time sifts through these immutable old screens.

14

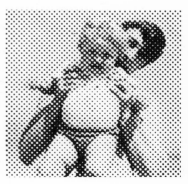

III. THE DANCE OF THE SOLIDS

ARGUMENT: In stanzas associated with allegory the actual atomic structure of solids unfolds. Metals, Ceramics, and Polymers. The conduction of heat, electricity, and light; nonsymmetry and magnetism. Solidity emerges as intricate and giddy.

All things are Atoms: Earth and Water, Air
    And Fire, all, *Democritus* foretold.
    Swiss *Paracelsus*, in's alchemic lair,
    Saw Sulphur, Salt, and Mercury unfold
    Amid Millennial hopes of faking Gold.
    Lavoisier dethroned Phlogiston; then
    Molecular Analysis made bold
    Forays into the gases: Hydrogen
Stood naked in the dazzled sight of Learned Men.

The Solid State, however, kept its grains
    Of Microstructure coarsely veiled until
    X-ray diffraction pierced the Crystal Planes
    That roofed the giddy Dance, the taut Quadrille
    Where Silicon and Carbon Atoms will
    Link Valencies, four-figured, hand in hand
    With common Ions and Rare Earths to fill
    The lattices of Matter, Salt or Sand,
With tiny Excitations, quantitively grand.

The *Metals*, lustrous Monarchs of the Cave,
    Are ductile and conductive and opaque
    Because each Atom generously gave
    Its own Electrons to a mutual Stake,
    A Pool that acts as Bond. The Ions take
    The stacking shape of Spheres, and slip and flow

When pressed or dented; thusly *Metals* make
A better Paper Clip than a Window,
Are vulnerable to Shear, and, heated, brightly glow.

Ceramic, muddy Queen of Human Arts,
    First served as simple Stone. Feldspar supplied
    Crude Clay; and Rubies, Porcelain, and Quartz
    Came each to light. Aluminum Oxide
    Is typical—a Metal close-allied
    With Oxygen ionically; no free
    Electrons form a lubricating tide,
    Hence, Empresslike, *Ceramics* tend to be
Resistant, porous, brittle, and refractory.

Prince *Glass*, *Ceramic*'s son, though crystal-clear,
    Is no wise crystalline. The fond Voyeur
    And Narcissist alike devoutly peer
    Into Disorder, the Disorderer
    Being Covalent Bondings that prefer
    Prolonged Viscosity and spread loose nets
    Photons slip through. The average *Polymer*
    Enjoys a Glassy state, but cools, forgets
To slump, and clouds in closely patterned Minuets.

The *Polymers*, those giant Molecules,
    Like Starch and Polyoxymethylene,
    Flesh out, as protein serfs and plastic fools,
    This Kingdom with Life's Stuff. Our time has seen
    The synthesis of Polyisoprene
    And many cross-linked Helixes unknown
    To *Robert Hooke;* but each primordial Bean
    Knew Cellulose by heart. *Nature* alone
Of Collagen and Apatite compounded Bone.

What happens in these Lattices when *Heat*
   Transports Vibrations through a solid mass?
   $T = 3Nk$ is much too neat;
   A rigid Crystal's not a fluid Gas.
   Debye in 1912 proposed Elas-
   Tic Waves called *phonons* that obey *Max Planck's*
   $E = hv$. Though amorphous Glass,
   Umklapp Switchbacks, and Isotopes play pranks
Upon his Formulae, *Debye* deserves warm Thanks.

Electroconductivity depends
   On Free Electrons: in Germanium
   A touch of Arsenic liberates; in blends
   Like Nickel Oxide, *Ohms* thwart Current. From
   Pure Copper threads to wads of Chewing Gum
   Resistance varies hugely. Cold and Light
   As well as "doping" modify the sum
   Of *Fermi* levels, Ion scatter, site
Proximity, and other Factors recondite.

Textbooks and Heaven only are Ideal;
   Solidity is an imperfect state.
   Within the cracked and dislocated Real
   Nonstoichiometric crystals dominate.
   Stray Atoms sully and precipitate;
   Strange holes, *excitons*, wander loose; because
   Of Dangling Bonds, a chemical Substrate
   Corrodes and catalyzes—surface Flaws
Help Epitaxial Growth to fix adsorptive claws.

White Sunlight, *Newton* saw, is not so pure;
   A Spectrum bared the Rainbow to his view.
   Each Element absorbs its signature:

Go add a negative Electron to
Potassium Chloride; it turns deep blue,
As Chromium incarnadines Sapphire.
Wavelengths, absorbed, are reëmitted through
Fluorescence, Phosphorescence, and the higher
Intensities that deadly *Laser Beams* require.

Magnetic Atoms, such as Iron, keep
Unpaired Electrons in their middle shell,
Each one a spinning Magnet that would leap
The *Bloch* Walls whereat antiparallel
Domains converge. Diffuse Material
Becomes *Magnetic* when another Field
Aligns domains like Seaweed in a swell.
How nicely microscopic forces yield,
In Units growing visible, the World we wield!

IV. THE PLAY OF MEMORY

ARGUMENT: The poet remembers and addresses those he has loved. Certain equations emerge from the welter, in which Walt Whitman swims. Arrows urge us on. Imagery from Canto II returns, enlarged. Sonnet to his father. Conception as climax of pointillism theme.

At the foot of the playground slide

FEET,

striking the dust,
had worn a trough
that after a rain
became a puddle.

Last night
lying listening to rain
myriads of points of sound
myriads

memory of girl—worker for McCarthy—came to door—zoftig—lent her my wife's bathing suit—she pinned it—she was smaller than my wife—pinned it to fit—the house upstairs hushed—velvety sense of summer dust—she came down—we went to beach—talked politics lying on pebbles—her skin so pale—bra too big so the curve of her breast was revealed nearly to the nipple—"If he ever got any real power it'd ruin him for me"—pebbles hurt her young skin—we came home—she took shower—should have offered to wash her back—passing me on way to the bathroom—skin—dawn-colored skin—eyes avoided—eye/I—I should have

offered to wash her back—dressed in her own cool clothes
she handed me back the bathing suit unpinned again—lovely
skin of her arms untanned from a summer of campaigning
by telephone—strange cool nerve taking a shower in mar-
ried man's wifeless home—the velvety summer dust waiting
to be stirred, to be loved, by the fan—left her by South
Green—"You'll be all right"—"Oh sure"—girls hitchhike
now—a silk-skinned harem drifting through this conscience-
stricken nation

CLEAN GENE

                    and empty arms
I made a note for this poem
                 in the dark
                        Where am I?
                              ALL
wrong, all wrong
            myriads
                   window mullions
                          dust motes
Sense of Many Things
                 what was being said through them?
S o m e t h i n g

          "huh?"

        also we
        used to
        play hop-
        scotch
        with a
        rubber heel ——→

23

⟶

1

2

3

4 5

6 7

8

9 10   *"Hey!"*

You who used to swing on the pavilion rafters
        showing me your underpants
you with whom I came six times in one night
                back from St. Thomas sunburned
in my haste to return
    my skin peeling from my chest like steamed wallpaper
my prick toward morning a battered miracle
            of response
and your good mouth wetter than any warm washrag
    and the walk afterwards toward the Park
        past Doubleday's packed with my books
your fucked-out insides airy in your smile
        and my manner a proud boy's
                        after some stunt
did you know you were showing me your underpants?
    did you know they said you laid
            beneath the pines by the poorhouse dam?
and in the Algonquin you
    in the persimmon nightie just down to your pussy

and your air of distraction
    your profile harassed against the anonymous wall
        that sudden stooping kiss
a butterfly on my glans
your head beat like a wing on the pillow
        your whimper in the car
you wiped blood from me with a Kleenex
    by the big abandoned barn I never drive past
                without suffering
you who outran me at fox-in-the-morning
    whom I caught on the steps of the Fogg
        the late games of Botticelli
you in your bed Ann in hers
    and the way we would walk to the window
        overlooking the bird sanctuary
our hands cool on each other's genitals
    have you forgotten?
we always exuded better sex than we had
    should I have offered to wash your back?
  you whose breast I soaped
        and you my cock, and your cunt
indivisible from the lather and huge as a purse and the mirror
    giving us back ourselves
        I said look because we were so beautiful and
you said "we're very ordinary"
    and in the Caribbean the night you knelt
to be taken from behind and we were entangled
        with the mosquito netting
and in the woods you let me hold your breasts
    your lipstick all flecked
the twigs dissolved in the sky above and I jerked off
    driving home alone onehanded
singing of you

you who demurely clenched
your thighs and came and might have snapped my neck
you who nursed me
and fed me dreams of Manhattan in the cloudy living-room
and rubbed my sore chest with VapoRub
        and betrayed me with my father
                and laughed it off
and betrayed me with your husband
                and laughed it off
and betrayed me beneath the pines
                and never knew I thought I knew
your underpants were ghostly gray and now
        you wear them beneath your nightie
                                and shy from my hug
        pubescent
        my daughter
who when I twirled you and would not stop bit my leg
        on West Thirteenth Street
you who lowered your bathing suit in the dunes
        your profile distracted against the sand
                your hips a table
        holding a single treat
your breasts hors d'oeuvres
you fed me tomatoes until I vomited
        because you wanted me to grow and you
said my writing was "a waste" about "terrible people"
        and tried to call me down from the tree
                for fear I'd fall
and sat outside nodding while I did toidy
        because I was afraid of ghosts
and said to me "the great thing about us is
        you're sure of the things I'm unsure about and
        I'm sure of the things you're unsure about"

and you blamed yourself for my colds
and my skin and my gnawing panic to excel, you
walked with me on Penn Street
the day I tried to sell cartoons to Pomeroy's
and they took our picture **LOANS**
Oh Mother above
our heads it said

LOANS

I think of you and mirrors:
the one that hung in the front hall
murky and flyspecked and sideways
and the little round one with which you
conducted arcane examinations by the bedside
I lying on the bed and not daring
look over the edge
I was a child and as an infant
I had cracked this mirror in a tantrum
it had a crack
it was a crack
O

MIRRORS ARE VAGINAS
and everywhere I go I plunge my gaze
into this lustrous openness
to see if I have grown
"Prodigal, you have given me love!
Therefore I to you give love!"
"O I am wonderful!
I cannot tell how my ankles bend"

"The smallest sprout shows
        there is really no death"
"And the pismire is equally perfect,
       and a grain of sand,
           and the egg of the wren"
"What is commonest, cheapest,
       nearest, easiest, is Me"

Given **M** = **V**
and sex as a "knowing";
    "knowing" = "seeing"

∴ **PENISES ARE EYES**

"his eyes shut and a bird flying below us he was shy all the
same I liked him like that morning I made him blush a little
when I got over him that way when I unbuttoned him and
took his out and drew back the skin it had a kind of eye in it"
Q. E. D.

and you who sat
       and so beautifully listened
your gray hair limpid and tense like a forest pool
"nor whence the cause of my faintest wish"
      listened as I too effortlessly talked
        after putting on my glasses
      (you called them my "magic eyes")
shielding my genitals (remember
      the Cocteau movie where he slashes an egg?

not to mention poor Gloucester's
   "vile jelly")
talked but never explicit anent sex
   "shy all the same"
trying to wheedle your love
   and after months and years
you pronounced at last:
    "are demonstrations of flying ability to this ugly
    earth-mother figure, successively incarnated in the
    husbands, rather than true relationships with the
            women"
"Oh,"

I said, "how sad if true"
   staggering out past the next patient
     in that room of old *Newsweeks*
      cured
sing   *oh*
  "adulterous offers made, acceptances,
      rejections with convex lips"
"Copulation is no more rank
     to me than death is"
"And mossy scabs of the worm fence,
     and heap'd stones, elder,
       mullen and poke-weed"
and Mother those three-way mirrors
    in Croll & Keck you
      buying me my year's jacket
my Joseph's coat
    I saw my appalling profile
and the bulge at the back of my head
    as if my brain were pregnant

"apart from the pulling and hauling stands what I am"
   I felt you saw me as a fountain spouting
gray pool unruffled as you listened to me
    telling cleverly how I loved the mail
how on Philadelphia Avenue I would lie
    in the hall with the flecked mirror
waiting for Mr. Miller
    to plop the mail through the slot
      spilling over me

MALE/MAIL

letter-slots are vaginas
    and stamps are semen swimming in the dark
      engraved with DNA
      "vile jelly"
    and mailboxes wait capaciously to be fucked
    throughout the town as I insomniac
      you pet
"To touch my person to some one else's
      is about as much as I can stand"
"And I know I am solid and round"
      "The well-taken photographs—
but your wife or friend close and solid in your arms?"

"I tighten her all night to my thighs and lips"

the bed of two beds in the cabin
    whose levels did not meet
the pine needles myriad about us
and the double-decker bunk
    so that mounting me you bumped your
             head
and the sleeping bag spread   ↓
on the lawn by the saltwater inlet   *ow*
    mosquitoes
    myriads

 . . . .
 . . . .
 . . . .
 . . . .
 . . . .

    scintillations of grass
    conversation of distant water
"The play of shine and shade
    on the trees as the supple boughs wag"
   What is pressing through?
    take me
"For every atom belonging to me,
    as good belongs to you"
rien
"And nothing, not God,
    is greater to one than one's self is"
a trente et six ans
"Behavior lawless as snow-flakes"
    having waited out numerous dead nights with lis-
       tening and with prayer
    having brought myself back from the dead with
       extravagant motions of the mind
the slide

       the puddle

              the clack of box hockey

                      the pavilion

many years later you

          sat on my lap at a class reunion

     your fanny was girdled and hard

a mother of four and I the father of four

         your body metallic with sex

    and I was so happy I stuttered

perhaps Creation is a stutter of the Void

            (I could revise the universe if I just knew math)

     I think it may all turn out to be an illusion

         the red shift merely travel fatigue

   and distance losing its value like inflated currency

        (physicists are always so comfortably talking

            about infinite flashlight beams

            and men on frictionless roller skates)

    and the atom a wrinkle that imagines itself

         and mass a factor of our own feebleness

"And to die is different from what any one supposed,

                 and luckier"

     and if my body is history   "the

        then my ego is Christ   ant's a

    and no inversion is too great for me   centaur

       no fate too special   in his

    a drowning man cannot pull   dragon

         himself out by his own hair (Barth) world"

and you above me in the bunk

     coming and crying, "Fuck, John!"

    all our broken veins displayed

the honey of your coming a humming bird's tongue

     an involuntary coo

                you pulled

je pense que

having inwardly revolved numerous Protestànt elements—
    screen doors, worn Bibles, rubber condoms that snap
    and hurt, playground grass that feet have beaten into a
    dusty fuzz, certain popsicle pleasures and hours of real
    reading, dental pain, the sociable rasp of Sunday drinks,
    the roses dozing, the children bored—
                    where you were always present
whose shampooed groin
                    held all I wished to know—
    dance, words!—
I deduced
    a late bloomer but an early comer
    my works both green and overripe
(Proust spurred me to imitation,
            the cars aswish on Riverside Drive,
and Kierkegaard held back the dark waters, but)

j'arrive à la pensée que

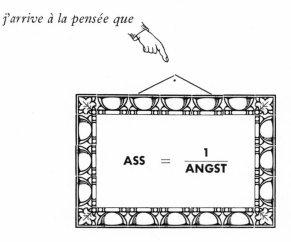

$$ASS = \frac{1}{ANGST}$$

            you pulled me up

33

I did fly
joy pulled a laugh from me
your hands, voice fluttered
"Is that funny? Is it?"
your nerves, voice tumbling
a two-body circus

thank you

the taint of performance

forgive me

your
face

your
tense
hand

your
good
sad
shoes

"In vain the mastodon retreats
beneath its own powder'd bones"

these dreadful nights of dust
    of discrete and cretin thoughts
        the mind searching for a virtue
    whereon to pillow and be oblivious
"The palpable is in its place,
           and the impalpable is in its place"
rummaging amid old ecstasies
         "your poetry began to go to pot
when you took up fucking housewives"
    a hitching-post for the heart
        the devil rides in circles

1 2 3 4 6 7 9 8 01

all wrong

wherever we turn we find a curved steel wall
        of previous speculation
and the water leaking from the main conduits
and the gauges rising,
        the needles shivering like whipped bitches
"The nearest gnat is an explanation,
        and a drop or motion of waves a key"
"I effuse my flesh in eddies,
        and drift in lacy jags"

try again

FATHER, as old as you when I was four,
I feel the restlessness of nearing death
But lack your manic passion to endure,
Your Stoic fortitude and Christian faith.
Remember, at the blackboard, factoring?
My life at midpoint seems a string of terms

35

In which an error clamps the hidden spring
Of resolution cancelling confirms.
Topheavy Dutchmen sundered from the sea,
Bewitched by money, believing in riddles
Syrian vagrants propagated, we
Incline to live by what the world belittles.
 God screws the lukewarm, slays the heart that faints,
 And saves His deepest silence for His saints.

I am a paper bag
     I am trying to punch my way out of
"Out of the dimness opposite equals advance—
    always substance and increase,

        always sex"

         let's go

"Always a knit of identity—
    always distinction—
       always a breed of life"
you who breathes beside me
     on Sparks Street spilled your cool nudity
across my eyes
      above the summer dust
    body of ivory I have marred, silk I have stretched

you came against me kneeling
        while a truck passed rumbling below
  and in Vermont   "a
the only souls in a square mile of mountain   garden
        the mantle lamps   is a
        the deck of cards   river
        the Unitarian paperbacks   flowing
        the spinning wheel gnawed by a porcupine   south"
we too had our violence
"The butcher-boy puts off his killing clothes"
    beside me like a sacrifice
mildly curious as to the knife
    did conceive
        in that square mile of wooded loneliness
a twinned point began to ravel
    you took me in
        "the fish-eggs are in their place"
most gracious   *merci*

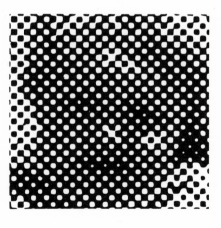

V. CONCLUSION

ARGUMENT: The poet strives to conclude, but his aesthetic of dots prevents him. His heroes are catalogued. World politics: a long view. Intelligent hedonistic advice. Chilmark Pond in August. He appears to accept, reluctantly, his own advice.

An easy Humanism plagues the land;
I choose to take an otherworldly stand.
The Archimedean point, however small,
Will serve to lift th' entire terrestrial Ball.
    Reality transcends itself within;
Atomically, all writers must begin.
The Truth arrives as if by telegraph:
One dot; two dots; a silence; then a laugh.
The rules inhere, and will not be imposed
Ab alto, as most Liberals have supposed.
    Praise *Kierkegaard,* who splintered *Hegel*'s creed
Upon the rock of Existential need;
Praise *Barth,* who told how saving Faith can flow
From Terror's oscillating Yes and No;
Praise *Henry Green,* who showed how lifetimes sift
Through gestures, glances, shrugs, and silly drift.
Praise *Disney,* for dissolving *Goofy*'s stride
Into successive stills our eyes elide;
And *Jan Vermeer,* for salting humble bread
With dabs of light, as well as bricks and thread.
Praise IBM, that boils the brain's rich stores
Down to a few electric either/ors;
Praise Pointillism, Calculus, and all
That turn the world infinitesimal:
The midget of the alphabet is I;
The Infinite is littleness heaped high.

All wrong, all wrong—throughout phenomena
Flashes the sword of Universal Law;
Elegant formulations sever Chance
From Cause, and clumsy Matter learns to dance.
A magnet subdivides into Domains
Till ratios are reached where Stasis reigns.
An insect's structure limits it; an Ant
Can never swell to be an Elephant.
The Demi-urge expands up to a rim
Where calculable cold collapses Him.

In human matters, too, Inductions act,
Cleave circumstance, and bare the general Fact.
Karl Marx and *Sigmund Freud* together show
Oppression alternates with Overthrow.
The proletarian Id combines its mass
With Superego's castellated class
To pinch the bourgeois Ego out of power:
The flag of Anarchy besports a flower;
The telescopic rifle and the cunt
Emblazon Urban Youth's united front.

The world boils over; Ho and Mao and Che
Blood-red inaugurate a brighter day.
Apocalypse is in; mad Eros drives
The continents upon a shoal of lives.
Awash with wealth, the fair Republic creaks,
While boilermen below enlarge the leaks;
What child is this, who cherishes still more
Confetti on the tilting ballroom floor?

Well, times are always desperate; this strange
Earth greets the old catastrophe of Change.
In bins of textbooks, holocausts lie stacked:
"No life was spared when Ghengis Khan attacked."

It little counts in History's level eye
Just how we copulate, or how we die.
Six million Jews will join the Congolese
King Leopold of Belgium cleared like trees,
And Hiroshima's epoch-making flash
Will fade as did the hosts of *Gilgamesh*.
The Judgment Day seems nigh to every age;
But History blinks, and turns another page.
Our lovely green-clad mother spreads her legs—
Corrosive, hairy, rank—and, shameless, begs
For Pestilence to fuck her if he can,
For War to come, and come again, again.
     The meanwhile, let us live as islanders
Who pluck what fruit the lowered branch proffers.
Each passing moment masks a tender face;
Nothing has had to be, but is by Grace.
Attend to every sunset; greet the dawn
That combs with spears of shade the glistening lawn.
Enjoy the slanting morning, upright noon,
Declining day, and swollen leprous moon.
Observe the trees, those clouds of breathing leaf;
Their mass transcends the insect's pointed grief.
The forest holds a thousand deaths, yet lives;
The lawn accepts its coat of bone and gives
Next spring a sweeter, graver tone of green.
Gladly the maple seed spins down, between
Two roots extends a tendril, grips beneath
The soil, and suffers the mower's spinning teeth.
Nothing is poorly made; nothing is dull:
The Crabgrass thinks itself adorable.
     Cherish your work; take profit in the task:
Doing's the one reward a Man dare ask.

The Wood confides its secrets to the plane;
The dovetail fits, and reconfirms the grain.
The white-hot writhing Steel is tonged and plunged,
A-sizzle, into Form, all flecks expunged.
The Linotyper leans above his keys,
And feathers down a ton of journalese;
Engraver and Apprentice, in their room
Of acid baths and photophobic gloom,
Transform to metal dots ten shades of gray,
And herald Everyman's beginning day.
    The Clergyman, beside the sighing bed,
Strains for a sign of credence from the dead;
The Lawyer eagle-eyed for Falsehood's glint,
The Doctor rapt for Angina's murmured hint,
The Biochemist analyzing sera,
The Astrophysicist alone with Lyra,
The Archaeologist with pick and brush,
The Nature-walker having spied a thrush—
Attentiveness! The pinpoint is the locus
Of Excellence in lands of softened focus.
    Applaud your Neighbor; admire his style
That grates upon you like a sawtooth file.
His trespasses resemble yours in kind;
He too is being crowded from behind.
Don't kill; or if you must, while killing, grieve.
Doubt not; that is, until you can't believe.
Don't covet Mrs. X; or if you do,
Make sure, before you leap, she covets you.
    Like meat upon the table, we will spoil:
Time is the troubled water; Faith, the oil.
The curse of Tempo regulates the dance;
To move necessitates Impermanence.

So flow, flow outward; *Heraclitus* saw,
In Nature's crystalline, the fluid flaw:
Our Guilt inheres in sheer Existing, so
Forgive yourself your death, and freely flow.

Transcendent Goodness makes elastic claims;
The merciful Creator hid His Aims.
Beware false Gods: the Infallible Man,
The flawless formula, the Five-Year Plan.
Abjure bandwagons; be shy of machines,
Charisma, ends that justify the means,
And oaths that bind the postulant to kill
His own self-love and independent Will.
A Mussolini leads to Hitler; hate
Apostles of the all-inclusive State.

Half-measures are most human; Compromise,
Inglorious and gray, placates the Wise.
By mechanistic hopes is Mankind vexed;
The Book of Life is margin more than text.
Ecclesiastes and our glands agree:
A time for love, for work, for sleep, for tea.
Organic music scores our ancient nerves:
Hark to its rhythm, conform to its curves.

All wrong? Advice, however sound, depends
Upon a meliorism Truth upends;
A certain Sinkingness resides in things.
The restless heart rejects what Fortune brings;
The Ego, too athletic, grows perverse
And muscle-builds by choosing worse and worse.
Our bones are prison-bars, our flesh is cells:
Where Suicide invites, Death-wish impels.
Earthquake, Diseases, Floods, Eruptions, Drought,

Black Comets, Starry Landslides, Wreck and Rout—
Beneath a cliff of vast Indifference
We light our frail fires, peg our poor tents.
The sleepless mouse-gray hours gnaw and stress:
"The Wisdom of the Earth is Foolishness."

   Yet morning here, by Chilmark Pond, is fair.
The water scintillates against the air,
The grassy earth spins seed from solar rage,
And patiently denies its awful age.
   I am another world, no doubt; no doubt
We come into this World from well without.
The seasons lessen; Summer's touch betrays
A tired haste, a cool autumnal trace.
The playground dust was richer, once, than loam,
And green, green as Eden, the slow path home;
No snows have been as deep as those my sled
Caressed to ice before I went to bed.
Perhaps Senility will give me back
The primitive rapport I lately lack.
   Adulthood has its comforts: these entail
Sermons and sex and receipt of the mail,
Elimination's homely paean, dreams'
Mad gaiety, avoidance of extremes,
The friendship of children, the trust of banks,
Thoracic pangs, a stiffness in the shanks,
Foretastes of death, the aftertaste of sin,
In winter, Whiskey, and in summer, Gin.
   The marsh gives way to Pond, to dunes, to Sea;
Cicadas call it good, and I agree.
At midpoint, center of a Hemisphere
Too blue for words, I've grown to love it here.

Earth wants me, it shall have me, yet not yet;
Some task remains, whose weight I can't forget,
Some package, anciently addressed, of praise,
That keeps me knocking on the doors of days.

  The time is gone, when *Pope* could ladle Wit
In couplet droplets, and decanter it.
Wordsworth's sweet brooding, *Milton*'s pride,
And *Tennyson*'s unease have all been tried;
Fin-de-siècle sickliness became
High-stepping Modernism, then went lame.
Art offers now, not cunning and exile,
But blank explosions and a hostile smile.

  Deepest in the thicket, thorns spell a word.
Born laughing, I've believed in the Absurd,
Which brought me this far; henceforth, if I can,
I must impersonate a serious man.

April–August 1968

44

Poems

FIREWORKS

These spasms and chrysanthemums of light
are like emotions
exploding under a curved night that corresponds
to the dark firmament within.

See, now, the libidinous flare,
spinning on its stick in vain resistance
to the upright ego and mortality's gravity;
behold, above, the sudden bloom,
turquoise, each tip a comet,
of pride—followed, after an empty bang,
by an ebbing amber galaxy, despair.

We feel our secrets bodied forth like flags
as wide as half the sky. Now
passions, polychrome and coruscating, crowd
one upon the other in a final fit,
a terminal display
that tilts the children's faces back in bleached dismay
and sparks an infant's crying in the grass.

They do not understand, the younger ones,
what thunderheads and nebulae,
what waterfalls and momentary roses fill
the world's one aging skull,
and are relieved when in a falling veil
the last awed outburst crumbles to reveal
the pattern on the playroom wall
of tame and stable stars.

LAMPLIGHT

Sent straight from suns
on slender stems
whose fangèd tendrils
leech the walls,
it sadly falls
on table tops
and barren floors
where rugs lie flat
as sunburnt crops.

Yet by this glow,
while daylight leans
outside the door
like an idle ax,
green voices wax,
red tongues thrust seeds
deep in the soil
of our harrowed needs,
and conversations grow.

HOME MOVIES

How the children have changed! Rapt we stare
 At flickering lost Edens where
 Pale infants, squinting, seem to hark
To their older selves laughing in the dark.

And then, by the trellis in some old Spring—
 The seasons are unaltering—
 We gather, smoother and less bald,
Innocently clowning, having been called

By the cruelly invisible cameraman.
 How silently time ran!
 We cannot climb back, nor can our friends,
To that calm light. The brief film ends.

THE ORIGIN OF LAUGHTER

(*after Desmond Morris*)

Hunched in the dark beneath his mother's heart,
The fetus sleeps and listens; dropped into light,
He seeks to lean his ear against the breast
Where the known rhythm holds its secret pace.

Slowly, slowly, through blizzards of dozing,
A face is gathered, starting with the eyes—
At first, quite any face; two painted dots
On cardboard stir a responsive smile. Soon
No face but one will serve: the mother's,
A mist, a cloud that clearly understands.

She teases him, pretends to let him drop.
He wants to cry but knows that she is good.
Out of this sudden mix, this terror rimmed
With necessary flesh, a laugh is born.

TOPSFIELD FAIR

Animals seem so sad to be themselves—
the turkey a turkey even to his wattle,
the rabbit with his pink, distinctly, eyes,
the prize steer humble in his stall.

What are they thinking, the pouter pigeons,
shaped like decadent ladies' hats,
jerking and staring in aisles of cages;
what does the mute meek monkey say?

Our hearts go out to them, then stop:
our fellows in mortality, like us
stiff-thrust into marvellous machines
tight-packed with chemical commands
to breathe, blink, feed, sniff, mate,
and, stuck like stamps in species, go out of date.

DOG'S DEATH

She must have been kicked unseen or brushed by a car.
Too young to know much, she was beginning to learn
To use the newspapers spread on the kitchen floor
And to win, wetting there, the words, "Good dog!
                                            Good dog!"

We thought her shy malaise was a shot reaction.
The autopsy disclosed a rupture in her liver.
As we teased her with play, blood was filling her skin
And her heart was learning to lie down forever.

Monday morning, as the children were noisily fed
And sent to school, she crawled beneath the youngest's bed.
We found her twisted and limp but still alive.
In the car to the vet's, on my lap, she tried

To bite my hand and died. I stroked her warm fur
And my wife called in a voice imperious with tears.
Though surrounded by love that would have upheld her,
Nevertheless she sank and, stiffening, disappeared.

Back home, we found that in the night her frame,
Drawing near to dissolution, had endured the shame
Of diarrhoea and had dragged across the floor
To a newspaper carelessly left there. *Good dog.*

DÉCOR

Brown dominates this bar
where men come to age:
the waiters Negro,
the whiskey unwatered,
the overheard voices from Texas,
the cigars and varnished wood.

Brown, the implication is,
is a shade of the soul,
the color of a man:
well-tanned and stained
to the innermost vein
as if life is a long curing.

CAMERA

Let me gaze, gaze forever
into that single, vaguely violet eye:
my fingertips dilate
the veiled pupil circumscribed
by crescent leaves of metal
overlapping, fine as foil, and oiled.

Let me walk, walk with its weight
as telling as gold, declaring
precious works packed tight:
the air is light,
all light, pure light alive
with the possibility of capture.

Let all, all be still until
the cleaver falls: I become female,
having sealed secure
in the quick clicked womb of utter black, bright semen
of a summer day, coiled fruit
of my eyes' axed rapture.

DREAM OBJECTS

Strangest is their reality,
their three-dimensional workmanship:
veined pebbles that have an underside,
maps one could have studied for minutes longer,
books we seem to read page after page.

If these are symbols cheaply coined
to buy the mind a momentary pardon,
whence this extravagance? Fine
as dandelion polls, they surface and explode
in the wind of the speed of our dreaming,

so that we awake with the sense
of having missed everything, tourists
hustled by bus through a land whose history
is our rich history, whose artifacts
were filed to perfection by beggars we fear.

THE ANGELS

They are above us all the time,
the good gentlemen, Mozart and Bach,
Scarlatti and Handel and Brahms,
lavishing measures of light down upon us,
telling us, over and over, there is a realm
above this plane of silent compromise.
They are around us everywhere, the old seers,
Matisse and Vermeer, Cézanne and Piero,
greeting us echoing in subway tunnels,
springing like winter flowers from postcards
Scotch-taped to white kitchen walls,
waiting larger than life in shadowy galleries
to whisper that edges of color
lie all about us innocent as grass.
They are behind us, beneath us,
the abysmal books, Shakespeare and Tolstoy,
the Bible and Proust and Cervantes,
burning in memory like leaky furnace doors,
minepits of honesty from which we escaped
with dilated suspicions. Love us, dead thrones,
sing us to sleep, awaken our eyes,
comfort with terror our mortal afternoons.

SUNSHINE ON SANDSTONE

Golden photon white on granulated red
  makes brown,
wall-broad in this instance,
  house-high:
splendiferous surface, the stucco
  worn bare
here and there, stones nicked, cracked,
  flecked, marked,
scored warmly, worn considerably, having
  wept rust,
borne whitewash, mortar, known weather,
  these spots
seem meditating irregularities:
  Lord's thoughts.

POMPEII

They lived, Pompeiians,
as installments of flesh in slots of stone;
they died in postures preserved,
by a ghoulish casting process, in the dank museum here.
Outside the gates, living Pompeiian men
peddle antique pornography.

One feels this place
was cursed before that noon in 79
when lunching gluttons found
their sturgeon mouths hot-stuffed with screaming ash.
There is little to admire but the fact
of preservation, and the plumbing.

The plumbing lingers
like a sour aftertaste—the loving conduits,
the phallic fountains, the three degrees,
so technically astute, of public bath. These Romans
lorded a world of well-enslaved liquids; pornography
became their monument.

ROMAN PORTRAIT BUSTS

Others in museums pass them by,
but I, I
am drawn like a maggot to meat
by their pupilless eyes
and their putrefying individuality.

They are, these Livias and Marcuses,
these pouting dead Octavias,
no two alike: never has art
so whorishly submitted
to the importunities of the real.

In good conscience one must admire
the drab lack of exaggeration,
the way each head,
crone's, consul's, or child's,
is neither bigger nor smaller than life.

Their eyes taste awful.
It is vile,
deliciously, to see them so
unsoftened by history, such
indigestible gristle.

AMOEBA

Mindless, meaning no harm,
it ingested me.
It moved on silent pseudopods
to where I was born, inert, and I
was inside.

Digestive acids burned my skin.
Enzymes nuzzled knees and eyes.
My ego like a conjugated verb
retained its root, a narrow fear
of being qualified.

Alas, suffixes swarmed.
I lost my mother's arms, my teeth,
my laugh, my protruding faith;
Reduced to the O of a final sigh,
in time I died.

SEAL IN NATURE

Seen from down the beach, the seal
seemed a polished piece of the rock he was on.
Closer approached, he became distinct
from the boat-shaped barnacled mineral mass,
twenty yards safe from shore, he had chosen
to be his pedestal—a living sculpture,
a Noguchi, an Arp, a Brancusi smoothed
from a flexible wood whose grain was hair,
whose gray was white in the abstract glisten,
and black where his curve demanded a shadow.

Sea his amphitheatre, the rippling mammal,
both water and stone, performed aloof wonders:
he wound the line of horizon on his nose,
and scratched his back with the top of his head,
and, twisting like a Möbius strip, addressed
the sky with a hollowing ululant howl
echoing empty epochs when,
in acres of basalt sown thick with steam,
spaced stars of life took antic shapes
and God was an undreamt dream.

THE AVERAGE EGYPTIAN
FACES DEATH

(*Based upon an Article in* Life)

Anubis, jackal-headed god
of mummification, will tenderly
eviscerate my corpse, oil it, salt it,
soothe it with unguent gods' tears and honey.

My soul will be a ba-bird,
a shadow, free to move in and out
of my muralled house,
though it's no pyramid.

In the court of Osiris the gods
will weigh my heart
for virtue; in the Field of Reeds
baboons worship Re,
and barley grows, and
beetle-headed Khepri, god of early morning,
kisses the misted canals.

Atum the creator has set
a smoky partition in the midst of things,
but the Nile flows through;
death has no other name than *ankh*, life.

Love Poems

NUDA NATENS

Anthea, your shy flanks in starlight
sank into the surf like thumbs into my heart.
Your untanned skin,
shaped like a bathing-suit,
lifted me thick from my thighs,
old Adam in air
above the cool ribs of sand.
My lust was a phosphor in a wide black wash,
and your quick neck the stem of a vase,
and your shoulders a crescent perilously balanced
where darkness was sliding on darkness.
You led me up, frightened with love,
up from the wet to where warm wind
bathed us in dust, and your embarrassed beauty
bent silver about your pudenda.

LOVE SONNET

In Love's rubber armor I come to you;
                                    b
                        oo
                                        b.
                    c,
                        d
                        c
                        d:
                    e
            f —
                e
                    f.
                            g
                        g.

CHLOË'S POEM

When Chloë flies on silken wings
   She pulls the sky itself along,
And every tugging moment brings
   The butterfly's request: "Be strong."
Her several mouths are graciousness;
   Her many hands, discovery:
A hurricane in each caress
   Is Chloë's way of treating me.

REPORT OF HEALTH

I

I am alone tonight.
The wrong I have done you
sits like a sore beneath my thumb,
burns like a boil on my heart's left side.
I am unwell.

My viscera, long clenched in love of you,
have undergone a detested relaxation.

There is, within, a ghostly maze
of phantom tubes and nodules where
those citizens, our passions, flit; and here,
like sunlight passing from a pattern of streets,
I feel your bright love leaving.

II

Another night. Today I am told,
dear friend, by another,
you seem happy and well.
Nothing could hurt me more.

How dare you be happy, you,
shaped so precisely for me,
my cup and my mirror—
how dare you disdain to betray,
by some disarray of your hair,
my being torn from you?

I would rather believe
that you knew your friend would come to me,
and so seemed well—
"not a hair / out of place"—
like an actress blindly hurling a pose
into the fascinated darkness.

As for me, you are still the eyes of the air.
I travel from point to point in your presence.
Each unattended gesture hopes to catch your eye.

III

I may not write again. My voice
goes nowhere. Dear friend,
don't let me heal. Don't
worry, I am well.
I am happy
to dwell in a world whose Hell I will:

the doorway hints at your ghost
and a tiger pounces on my heart;
the lilac bush is a devil
inviting me into your hair.

MY CHILDREN AT THE DUMP

The day before divorce, I take my children
on this excursion;
they are enchanted by
a wonderland of discard where
every complicated star cries out
to be a momentary toy.

To me, too, the waste seems wonderful.
Sheer hills of television tubes, pale lakes
of excelsior, landslides
of perfectly carved carpentry-scraps,
sparkplugs like nuggets, cans iridescent
as peacock plumes, an entire lawnmower . . .
all pluck at my instinct to conserve.

I cannot. These things
were considered, and dismissed
for a reason. But my children
wander wondering among tummocks of junk
like stunted starvelings cruelly set free
at a heaped banquet of food too rich to eat.
I shout, "Don't touch the broken glass!"

The distant metal delicately rusts.
The net effect is floral: a seaward wind
makes flags of cellophane and upright weeds.
The seagulls weep; my boys bring back
bent tractors, hoping what some other child
once played to death can be revived by them.

No. I say, "No." I came to add
my fragments to this universe of loss,
purging my house, ridding a life
no longer shared of remnants.
My daughter brings a naked armless doll,
still hopeful in its dirty weathered eyes,
and I can only tell her, "Love it now.
Love it now, but we can't take it home."

WASHINGTON

Diagonal white city dreamed by a Frenchman—
the *nouveau* republic's Senecan pretension
populated by a grid of blacks—
after midnight your taxi-laced streets
entertain noncommittal streetlight shadows
and the scurry of leaves that fall still green.

Site, for me, of a secret parliament
of which both sides agreed to concede
and left the issue suspended in brandy,
I think of you longingly, as a Yankee
longs for Lee, sorry to have won,
or as Ho Chi Minh mourns for Johnson.

My capital, my alabaster Pandemonium,
I rode your stunned streets with a groin
as light and docile as a baby's wrist,
guilt's senators laughing in my skull's cloakroom,
my hurried heart corrupt with peace,
with love of my country, of cunt, and of sleep.

FELLATIO

It is beautiful to think
that each of these clean secretaries
at night, to please her lover, takes
a fountain into her mouth
and lets her insides, drenched in seed,
flower into landscapes:
meadows sprinkled with baby's breath,
hoarse twiggy woods, birds dipping, a multitude
of skies containing clouds, plowed earth stinking
of its upturned humus, and small farms each
with a silver silo.

SUBWAY LOVE

Negress serene though underground,
what weddings in northward Harlem
impressed upon you this cameo
stamp of stoic repose?
Beauty should never be bored
with being beautiful.

Stark lights shatter at our speed.
Couplings cluck, the darkness yells.
The child beside you sidles in
and out of sleep, and I,
poor sooty white man scarcely visible,
try not to stare.

O loveliness blind to itself:
sockets thumbed from clay wherein
eyelids are petals of shadow,
cheekbones and jawbone whose carriage
is of a proud rider in velvet,
lips where eleven curves live.

Eurydice, come follow me,
my song is silent, listen:

I'll hold your name in love so high
oceans of years will leave it dry;
mountains of time will not begin
to move a moment of your skin.

The doors gape wide at Fifty-ninth.
The kiosk steps are black with blood.
I turn and find,
rebuked by light,
you gone, Negress serene,
tugged northward into night.

MINORITY REPORT

My beloved land,
here I sit in London
    overlooking Regent's Park
    overlooking my new Citroën } both green,
exiled by success of sorts.
I listen to Mozart
  in my English suit and weep,
    remembering a Swedish film.
But it is you,
  really you I think of:
    your nothing streetcorners
    your ugly eateries
    your dear barbarities
    and vacant lots
(Br'er Rabbit demonstrated:
    freedom is made of brambles).
They say over here you are choking
  to death on your cities and slaves,
    but they have never smelled dry grass,
    smoked Kools in a drugstore,
    or pronounced a flat "a," an honest "r."
Don't read your reviews,
A ✩ M ✩ E ✩ R ✩ I ✩ C ✩ A:
you are the only land.

Light Verse

SOME FRENCHMEN

Monsieur Etienne de Silhouette*
   Was slim and uniformly black;
His profile was superb, and yet
   He vanished when he turned his back.

Humane and gaunt, precise and tall
   Was Docteur J. I. Guillotin;†
He had one tooth, diagonal
   And loose, which, when it fell, spelled *fin*.

André Marie Ampère,‡ a spark,
   Would visit other people's homes
And gobble volts until the dark
   Was lit by his resisting ohms.

Another type, Daguerre (Louis),§
   In silver salts would soak his head,
Expose himself to light, and be
   Developed just in time for bed.

* 1709–1767
† 1738–1814
‡ 1775–1836
§ 1789–1851

FAREWELL TO THE
SHOPPING DISTRICT OF ANTIBES

Next week, alas, BOULANGERIE
Will bake *baguettes,* but not for me;
The windows will be filled, although
I'm gone, with brandy-laced *gâteaux.*

TABAC, impervious, will vend
Reynos to others who can spend
Trois francs (moins dix centimes) per pack—
Forget me not, *très cher* TABAC!

Grim BOIS & CHARBONS & MAZOUT
Will blacken someone else's suit,
And FLEURS will romance with the air
As if I never had been there.

ALIMENTATION won't grieve
As it continues, *sans* my leave,
To garland *oignons,* peddle *pommes,*
And stack *endives* till kingdom come.

La mer will wash up on the sand
Les poissons morts regardless, and
JOURNAUX will ask, though I'm away,
"UN AUTRE MARI POUR B.B.?"

EXPOSÉ

LE CHAMP MAGNÉTIQUE DE VÉNUS
EST EXTRÊMEMENT FAIBLE
—*Headline in* Le Monde

Le Monde regrets it must report—
   In simple duty to the nation,
      And favoring no clique or faction—
      That Venus' powers of attraction,
When measured coolly, fall far short
   Of their much-vaunted reputation.

"*Extrêmement*"—harsh word, but then
   Le monde, it is a brutal planet,
      Unsentimental, unromantic.
      Poor *faible* Venus may be frantic
To be unmasked, but mundane men
   Have hearts of unmagnetic granite.

Released from her faint faded spell,
   Where shall we iron filings gather?
      Pale Mars is cold, Uranus gassy,
      And Saturn hopelessly *déclassé;*
Perhaps our lodestone lies in Hell.
   I still am drawn to Venus, rather.

THE AMISH

The Amish are a surly sect.
They paint their bulging barns with hex
Designs, pronounce a dialect
Of Deutsch, inbreed, and wink at sex.

They have no use for buttons, tea,
Life insurance, cigarettes,
Churches, liquor, Sea & Ski,
Public power, or regrets.

Believing motors undivine,
They bob behind a buggied horse
From Paradise to Brandywine,
From Bird-in-Hand to Intercourse.

They think the Devil drives a car
And wish Jehovah would revoke
The licensed fools who travel far
To gaze upon these simple folk.

AIR SHOW

(*Hanscom Field, Bedford, Mass.*)

In shapes that grow organic and bizarre
Our Air Force ramifies the forms of war.
The stubby bomber, dartlike fighter yield
To weirder beasts caught browsing on this field,
With wry truncated wings, anteater snouts,
And burnished bellies full of ins and outs.
  Caressing curves of wind, the metal smiles
And beds the pilot down in sheets of dials.
Eggheaded, strapped, and sucking gas, he roars
To frozen heights all other life abhors,
Where, having left his dirty sound behind,
In pure blue he becomes pure will and mind.
  These planes, articulate in every part,
Outdo the armor-forger's Tuscan art—
The rivets as unsparingly displayed
As pearls upon a chasuble's brocade,
The wiring bundled thick, like chordate brains,
The posing turbine balanced grain by grain,
The silver skin so stencilled it amounts
To an encyclical of do's and don't's.
  Our dollars! Dumb, like muzhiks come from far
To gaze upon the trappings of a czar,
Their sweat turned into gems and cold faïence,
We marvel at our own extravagance:
No mogul's wasteful lust was half so wide
And deep as this democracy's quick pride.

POSTCARDS FROM SOVIET CITIES

Moscow

Gold onions rooted in the sky
Grow downward into sullen, damp
Museums where, with leaden eye,
Siberian tourists dumbly tramp.

The streets are wide as silences.
The cobblestones between the GUM
And Kremlin echo—an abyss
Lies sealed within a giant room.

The marble box where Lenin sleeps
Receives the Tartar gaze of those
Who come from where Far Russia keeps
Her counsels wrapped in deadening snows.

St. Basil's, near at hand, erects
The swirlings that so charmed the Czar
He blinded both the architects
To keep such beauty singular.

Leningrad

"To build a window on the west"
Great Peter came to Neva's mouth
And found a swamp, which he oppressed
With stones imported from the south.

The city, subtly polychrome
(Old ochre, green, and dull maroon),
Can make Italians feel at home
Beneath the tilted arctic noon.

The Palace holds, pistachio,
A wilderness of treasure where
The ghosts of plump czarinas go
On dragging diamonds up the stair.

Suburban acres of the dead
Memorialize the Siege, a hell
Of blackened snow and watered bread.
Some couples Twist in our hotel.

Kiev

Clutching his cross, St. Vladimir
Gazes with eyes that seem to grieve
Across the sandy Dnieper, where
He baptized godforsaken Kiev.

Now deconverted trolleys turn
Around the square, emitting sparks.
The churches, cold as old snow, burn
With gilt above the poplar parks.

Beneath the earth, in catacombs,
Dried patriarchs lie mummified;
Brocaded silk enmeshed with bones
Offends our trim, mascaraed guide,

Who, driving homeward, gestures toward
The ruins of Moussorgsky's Gate—
Like some old altar, unrestored,
Where peasant women supplicate.

Tbilisi

Rich Georgian farmers send their sons
(Black-haired, with pointed stares and feet)
To town for educations—
They loiter laughing on the street.

A "working" church: its inside smells
Of tallow, mold, incense, and chrism.
The long-haired priest, wax-pallid, sells
His candles with a shopgirl's grimace.

The poets, overhonored, toast
Themselves with liquid syllables;
The alphabet is strange. They boast
Their tongue is older than their hills.

Instead of Stalin, who indulged
His native land with privilege,
A blank steel woman, undivulged
By name, surmounts the once-walled ridge.

Yerevan

Armenia, Asia's waif, has here
At last constructed shelter proof

Against all Turkish massacre.
A soft volcanic rock called *tuf*

Carves easily and serves to be
The basis of the boulevards
That lead from slums of history
Into a future stripped of swords.

The crescent-shaped hotel is rose
And looks toward Lenin Square and tan
Dry mountains down which power flows
From turbines lodged in Lake Sevan.

Mount Ararat, a conscience, floats
Cloudlike, in sight but unpossessed,
For there, where Noah docked his boat,
Begins the brutal, ancient West.

POEM FOR A FAR LAND

Russia, most feminine of lands,
  Breeder of stupid masculinity,
Only Jesus understands
  Your interminable virginity.

Raped, and raped, and raped again,
  You rise snow-white, the utter same,
With tender birches and ox-eyed men
  Willing to suffer for your name.

Though astronauts distress the sky
  That mothers your low, sad villages,
Your vastness yearns in sympathy
  Between what was and that which is.

ANTIGUA

The wind, transparent, cannot displace
  The vertical search of sun for skin.
The colonel's fine-veined florid face
  Has bloomed though sheltered deep within
His shining hat's mauve shade. His eyes
  Glare bluer than the coral-bleached
  Soft sea that feebly nags the beach
And hones its scimitar with sighs.

His wife, in modest half-undress,
  Swings thighs pinched red between the sea
  And sky, and smiles, serenely free
Of subcutaneous distress.
Above, sere cliffs attend their hike,
  And colored scraps give tattered hints
Of native life, and, higher, like
  A flaw in glass, an airplane glints.

AZORES

Great green ships
    themselves, they ride
at anchor forever;
    beneath the tide

huge roots of lava
    hold them fast
in mid-Atlantic
    to the past.

The tourists, thrilling
    from the deck,
hail shrilly pretty
    hillsides flecked

with cottages
    (confetti) and
sweet lozenges
    of chocolate (land).

They marvel at
    the dainty fields
and terraces
    hand-tilled to yield

the modest fruits
    of vines and trees
imported by
    the Portuguese:

a rural landscape
    set adrift
from centuries ago;
    the rift

enlarges.
    The ship proceeds.
Again the constant
    music feeds

an emptiness astern,
    Azores gone.
The void behind, the void
    ahead are one.

VOW

(On Discovering Oneself Listed on the Back of a
Concert Program as a "Museum Friend of Early Music")

May I forever a Muse-
um Friend of Early Music be;
May I, no, never cease to thrill
When three-stringed rebecs thinly trill,
Or fail to have a lumpish throat
When crumhorns bleat their fuzzy note.
I'll often audit, with *ma femme,*
Duets of psaltery and shawm;
Cross-flutes of pre-Baroque design
Shall twit our eardrums as we dine,
And Slavic guslas will, forsooth,
In harsh conjunction with the crwth
(Which is a kind of Welsh vielle,
As all us Friends know very well),
Lull both of us to sleep. My love,
The keirnines (Irish harps) above
Tune diatonically, and lyres
Augment august celestial choirs
That plan to render, when we die,
"Lamento di Tristano" by
Anonymous. With holy din
Recorder angels will tune us in
When we have run our mortal race
From sopranino to contrabass.

MISS MOORE AT ASSEMBLY

(Based, with a derived scrupulosity, upon an item in The
New York Times, *describing Marianne Moore's lecture
appearance before the students of a Brooklyn high school)*

A "chattering, gum-snapping audience"
  held rapt by poetess, hat
    tricorn, "gigantic white orchid
fluttering at her shoulder"—that
    suffices, in mid-
century, to tax one's fittingness's sense.

But why? . . . Birds heard Francis. Who else could come
  to Eastern District High School
    ("slum," "bubble-gum-snapping") and stand—
tobacco-eschewer but Bol-
    lingen-Prize-winner—and
say, "I've always wanted to play a snare drum"?

SEA KNELL

Pulsating Tones in Ocean
Laid to Whale Heartbeats
—*The Times*

There is a rapture on the lonely shore,
There is society, where none intrudes,
By the deep sea, and music in its roar . . .
—*Byron*

I wandered to the surfy marge
    To eavesdrop on the surge;
The ocean's pulse was slow and large
    And solemn as a dirge.

"Aha," mused I, "the beat of Time,
    Eternally sonorous,
Entombed forever in the brine,
    A fatal warning for us."

"Not so!" bespoke a jolly whale
    Who spouted into view,
"That pulsing merely proves I'm hale
    And hearty, matey, too!

"Rejoice, my lad—my health is sound,
    The very deeps attest!
It permeates the blue profound
    And makes the wavelets crest!"

With that, he plunged in sheer excess
    Of spirits. On the shore,
I harkened with an ear much less
    Byronic than before.

OMEGA

This little lightweight manacle whereby
My wrist is linked to flux and feels time fly,
This constant bracelet with so meek a jewel
Shall prove at last implacable and cruel
And like a noose jerk taut, and hold me still,
And add me to the unseen trapper's kill.

IN EXTREMIS

I saw my toes the other day.
I hadn't looked at them for months.
Indeed, they might have passed away.
And yet they were my best friends once.

When I was small, I knew them well.
I counted on them up to ten
And put them in my mouth to tell
The larger from the lesser. Then

I loved them better than my ears,
My elbows, adenoids, and heart.
But with the swelling of the years
We drifted, toes and I, apart.

Now, gnarled and pale, each said, *j'accuse!*—
I hid them quickly in my shoes.

ON THE INCLUSION
OF MINIATURE DINOSAURS
IN BREAKFAST CEREAL BOXES

A post-historic herbivore,
I come to breakfast looking for
A bite. Behind the box of Brex
I find *Tyrannosaurus rex*.

And lo! beyond the Sugar Pops,
An acetate *Triceratops*.
And here! across the Shredded Wheat,
The spoor of *Brontosaurus* feet.

Too unawake to dwell upon
A model of *Iguanodon*,
I hide within the Raisin Bran;
And thus begins the dawn of *Man*.

THE NAKED APE

*(Following, Perhaps All Too Closely,
Desmond Morris's Anthropological Revelations)*

The dinosaur died, and small
   Insectivores (how gruesome!) crawled
From bush to tree, from bug to bud,
   From spider-diet to forest fruit and nut,
Developing bioptic vision and
     The grasping hand.

These perfect monkeys then were faced
   With shrinking groves; the challenged race,
De-Edenized by glacial whim,
   Sent forth from its arboreal cradle him
Who engineered himself to run
     With deer and lion—

The "naked ape." Why naked? Well,
   Upon those meaty plains, that *veldt*
Of prey, as pellmell they competed
   With cheetahs, hairy primates overheated;
Selection pressure, just though cruel,
     Favored the cool.

Unlikeliest of hunters, nude
   And weak and tardy to mature,
This ill-cast carnivore attacked,
   With weapons he invented, *in a pack*.
The tribe was born. To set men free,
     The family

Evolved; monogamy occurred.
  The female—sexually alert
Throughout the month, equipped to have
  Pronounced orgasms—perpetrated love.
The married state decreed its *lex*
    Privata: sex.

And Nature, pandering, bestowed
  On virgin ears erotic lobes
And hung on women hemispheres
  That imitate their once-attractive rears:
A social animal disarms
    With frontal charms.

All too erogenous, the ape
  To give his lusts a decent shape
Conceived the cocktail party where
  Unmates refuse to touch each other's hair
And make small "grooming" talk instead
    Of going to bed.

He drowns his body scents in baths
  And if, in some conflux of paths,
He bumps another, says, "Excuse
  Me, *please*." He suffers rashes and subdues
Aggressiveness by making fists
    And laundry lists,

Suspension bridges, aeroplanes,
  And charts that show biweekly gains
And losses. Noble animal!
  To try to lead on this terrestrial ball,
With grasping hand and saucy wife,
    The upright life.

A Note About the Author

John Updike was born in 1932 in Shillington, Penn-
sylvania, and attended Harvard College and the
Ruskin School of Drawing and Fine Arts in Oxford,
England. From 1955 to 1957 he was a staff member
of *The New Yorker*, to which he has contributed
stories, essays, and poems. He is the author of five
novels and lives with his wife and four children in
Ipswich, Massachusetts.

A Note on the Type

The text of this book was set on the Linotype in
JANSON, a recutting made direct from type cast from
matrices long thought to have been made by the
Dutchman Anton Janson, who was a practicing
type founder in Leipzig during the years 1668–87.
However, it has been conclusively demonstrated
that these types are actually the work of Nicholas
Kis (1650–1702), a Hungarian, who most probably
learned his trade from the master Dutch type
founder Dirk Voskens. The type is an excellent
example of the influential and sturdy Dutch types
that prevailed in England up to the time William
Caslon developed his own incomparable designs
from these Dutch faces.

*This book was composed, printed, and bound
by Kingsport Press, Inc., Kingsport, Tennessee.*